STUDY GUIDE

Sermon on
the Mount

Sinclair B. Ferguson

LIGONIER MINISTRIES

Renew your Mind.

LIGONIER.ORG | 800-435-4343

1

Life in the Kingdom

INTRODUCTION

Jesus Christ preached with the authority of the promised coming King. In this introductory lesson, Dr. Ferguson places the Sermon on the Mount in the context of Matthew's gospel and summarizes its content and implications.

LESSON OBJECTIVES

1. To provide context for the Sermon on the Mount
2. To outline the major points of the Sermon on the Mount
3. To apply those points to the lives of believers

SCRIPTURE READING

From that time Jesus began to preach, saying, "Repent, for the kingdom of heaven is at hand."

—Matthew 4:17

LECTURE OUTLINE

A. The Sermon on the Mount must be understood in the context of what comes before it in Matthew's gospel.

1. Jesus presented Himself to be baptized.
    a. Jesus was baptized at the age of thirty.
    b. The Father identified Jesus as the Suffering Servant (Isa. 42:1) and the King to whom the Father would say, "Ask of me, and I will give you the nations for your inheritance" (Ps. 2:7–8).
2. Matthew's gospel begins and ends with the notion that "Jesus is the King."
    a. Matthew's genealogy tells us that Jesus is a descendant of King David.
    b. The prophecies about Jesus that Matthew highlights are prophecies about a coming King.

    c. Matthew ends his gospel with the words of Jesus, "All authority in heaven and on earth has been given to me" (Matt. 28:18).

    d. Jesus begins His public ministry by announcing the kingdom of God and the necessity to respond in repentance and faith (Matt. 4:17).

3. Jesus not only announces the presence of the kingdom but also displays the power of the kingdom.

    a. Jesus gains the power to set men and women free by overcoming the devil's temptations in the wilderness, and so heals the sick, the blind, and the demon possessed.

    b. Jesus reveals the power of the kingdom by the way he calls people into it; the first disciples immediately leave their nets to follow Him.

    c. Jesus has the authority to heal, to call, and to deliver—all allegiance is owed to Him, and diseases and evil spirits flee from His presence.

    d. The miracles of Jesus are momentary flashes of His final kingdom.

4. Jesus wants to teach His disciples what it is to live in the kingdom of God.

    a. Jesus has brought His disciples from darkness to light, but because the light is not shining fully and finally, His disciples must learn what it is to live in a fallen world.

B. The chapters of the Sermon on the Mount can each be summarized with one word.

1. The first chapter of the Sermon on the Mount can be summarized by the word *fulfillment*, as fulfillment comes through Jesus Christ.

    a. Jesus fulfills the prophecies and promises of the Old Testament.

    b. Jesus brings fulfillment to broken and bruised lives.

    c. Jesus fills His people full of life that is lived for the glory of God.

2. Jesus wants to teach us the difference between a life lived with Him and a life lived without Him.

    a. The blessings of the Christian are altogether different than the blessings of the world and reverse the standards of the world.

    b. The kingdom transforms people in such a way that they become different from those around them.

    c. The impact of a transformed life means that—like Jesus in all His compassion, tenderness, and miraculous works—those who follow Him will be persecuted (2 Peter 4:12).

    d. The righteousness of Christians goes deeper than that of the scribes and Pharisees, because Jesus teaches us the proper role of the law and enables us to keep it.

3. The next chapter of the Sermon on the Mount can be summarized by the word *Father.*

    a. Jesus teaches us that by being brought into the kingdom we are brought to know the heavenly Father.

    b. Knowing the heavenly Father is the key to living in the kingdom of God.

4. The last chapter of the Sermon on the Mount can be summarized by the word *judgment*.
   a. Jesus teaches His disciples how the transformed life changes the way they make judgments and decisions.
   b. Disciples' lives must ultimately be built on Jesus Christ.

C. The Sermon on the Mount ends by underlining the authority with which Jesus preached.
   1. There is a sense that the King has come.
   2. The big question is how will people respond.
   3. The rest of Matthew's gospel continues with some who respond in faith and others who respond in unbelief.

D. There are four primary applications to draw from this brief introduction to the Sermon on the Mount.
   1. The first application is that the different life that Jesus speaks of must have a supernatural origin.
      a. Many people claim to love the Sermon on the Mount because they are vaguely familiar with its content but do not truly know Jesus.
      b. The Sermon on the Mount is often misunderstood and does not drive people to their knees in awareness of their need and inability.
      c. Many people respond to the new life that Jesus teaches about through the gospel by saying, "I am going to try to do better."
      d. Jesus makes it plain that we cannot work out a new life for ourselves; we need the supernatural work of God's grace to see, understand, and enter the kingdom (John 3:3).
   2. The second application is that Jesus speaks about a transformation that goes to the very roots of our lives.
      a. Throughout our lives as Christians, Christ leads us deeper and deeper, exposing the hidden sins of our lives.
      b. The evangelical church has wrongly emphasized health, wealth, and happiness in order to attract the world to the life that Jesus creates.
      c. Jesus is rather concerned with deconstructing our lives to reveal the power of the gospel so that we would be different to the point of being like Him, even in the opposition He faced.
   3. The third application is that the transformation that Jesus creates in us is a life-long transformation of repentance.
      a. The first thesis of Martin Luther's Ninety-Five Theses: "When our Lord Jesus said, 'Repent,' He meant that the whole of the Christian life should be repentance."
   4. The fourth application is that the transformation of the Christian life only takes place when we bow to the authority of the Lord Jesus Christ.

STUDY QUESTIONS

1. Matthew's gospel begins and ends with the notion that Jesus is _____ .
    a. Prophet
    b. Priest
    c. King
    d. All of the above

2. The Father's words that identified Christ at His baptism as the Suffering Servant and King are references to the Psalms and _____ .
    a. Daniel
    b. Isaiah
    c. Ezekiel
    d. Jeremiah

3. Christ's first disciples left their nets because they were smart enough to recognize Christ's authority.
    a. True
    b. False

4. The first section of the Sermon on the Mount can be summarized by the word _____ .
    a. Father
    b. Fulfillment
    c. Judgment
    d. Transformation

5. Jesus abolishes the role of the law because He has fulfilled the law.
    a. True
    b. False

6. Jesus teaches us that the Christian life will be _____ .
    a. Supernatural in origin
    b. Deeply transformative
    c. Lifelong
    d. All of the above

DISCUSSION QUESTIONS

1. What significance did Christ's temptation in the wilderness have for His public ministry?

2. How does the Sermon on the Mount present the countercultural Christian life?

3. How does a message that only emphasizes health, wealth, and happiness undermine the gospel?

4. In what way is the Sermon on the Mount commonly misread?

2

The Beatitudes

INTRODUCTION

Jesus begins the Sermon on the Mount by defining the transformed life. In this lesson, Dr. Ferguson describes the personal characteristics of the Christian and how others will be able to recognize Jesus Christ through them.

LESSON OBJECTIVES

1. To make the logical connections from one beatitude to the next that define what it is to be a Christian
2. To nurture an understanding of the Christian life as one that reflects Christ to the world

SCRIPTURE READING

But the meek shall inherit the land, and delight themselves in an abundance of peace.

—Psalm 37:11

Then they left the presence of the council, rejoicing that they were counted worthy to suffer dishonor for the name.

—Acts 5:41

LECTURE OUTLINE

A. Jesus steps forward to begin His ministry in order to deal with the problems of our guilt and bondage.

1. Our guilt is ultimately before God, and we are in bondage not only to sin but also to Satan.
2. Christ is symbolically baptized into our sins at His baptism.
   a. The waters in which people had symbolically washed away their sins are poured over Jesus, and Jesus will fulfill this baptism on the cross.

      b. Jesus deals with our guilt so that we may become children of the heavenly Father.

3. Jesus underwent temptation in the wilderness in order to deal with our bondage.
    a. Unlike the temptations that come to us naturally, Jesus went as the Son of God to temptation in order to overcome the evil one.
    b. Jesus was tempted by the devil's promise to give Him the kingdoms of the world, which is what Jesus had come into the world to gain.
    c. Jesus indicated His willingness to deal with our guilt and rescue the kingdoms of the world through the way of the cross by not yielding to the temptations of the devil.
    d. Jesus defeated the devil in the wilderness and ushered in the new powers of the kingdom.

B. The Sermon on the Mount can be called "Christian Living 101."
    1. The Sermon on the Mount begins a series of teaching blocks unique to the book of Matthew.
       a. Matthew is divided into teaching blocks about the nature of the kingdom, how it works, how it will come, and how people will live in it.
       b. Jesus is teaching the most fundamental principles of what it means to be a Christian.
    2. The Sermon of the Mount does not begin by telling us what we are to do as Christians but by telling us the blessedness of what we are as Christians.
       a. Being is the foundation for doing in the Christian life.

C. There are important points to highlight about how Jesus describes the characteristics of citizens of the kingdom.
    1. The descriptions Jesus gives are descriptions of God's people that we find in various parts of the Old Testament.
       a. The promises scattered throughout the Old Testament are being brought together in the new life of the citizens of the kingdom.
       b. Jesus is quoting the Old Testament when He declares, "Blessed are the meek, because they will inherit the earth" (Ps. 37:11).
       c. Jesus has come to bring fulfillment (John 10:10), so the Beatitudes are characterized by contrasts underlining the fact that in order to be filled with Him, you need to be emptied of yourself.
    2. The Beatitudes reverse the values of the world in a way that is countercultural.
       a. It is the poor who are blessed, the meek who inherit the earth, and those who mourn who are comforted.
       b. The values of the world devalue the values of God.
    3. The countercultural transformation brings us into a world in which there is conflict and persecution.

a.   The Beatitudes end by emphasizing this fact.

b.   The Apostle Peter struggled with the desire to have the Christian life without opposition, persecution, and pain.

c.   Peter would later understand that Christians should expect to experience the same opposition that Jesus experienced (1 Peter 4:12).

4.   The Beatitudes are a description of Jesus Christ and reveal to us who we are in Him.

a.   Jesus is the One who mourned, the One who was poor in spirit, the One who was meek, and the One who was persecuted.

b.   The Beatitudes are really describing what it is to become like Christ.

c.   He is the blessed One, and in Him we will experience every spiritual blessing, even if it comes with suffering and persecution.

D.   The Beatitudes have a natural flow that logically connects them to one another.

1.   We need to become poor in spirit to enter the kingdom; we learn to be sorry for our sins.

2.   We are then able to understand what it is to mourn and be blessed, and in mourning, our pride is demolished as we begin to understand meekness.

3.   God works in us new ambitions, tastes, affections; we begin to love different things and different people; we begin to love the church.

4.   In being transformed, we begin to hunger and thirst for righteousness, and as we long for righteousness, we become merciful.

a.   We know firsthand what it is to receive mercy.

5.   Our hearts then become purified, and we begin to see God as the God of Peace.

a.   As He reconciled us to Himself in Christ, we seek to be reconciled to others and desire them to experience the same fellowship in Christ.

b.   We have physical expressions of our peace with God through Jesus Christ at the Lord's Supper.

c.   Some people claim to want peace in this world yet spend their lives rejecting God's desire that they should have peace with Him.

d.   Christians, on the other hand, are instinctively peacemakers.

6.   When persecution comes on account of following Christ, we should also instinctively understand that we are blessed.

a.   A natural response to ridicule and persecution is to fight back, but if we suffer for Christ, there is great joy in the realization that there must be something about us that reminds others of Him (Acts 5:41).

b.   We are also blessed because of our resolve to trust the Lord through persecution.

E.   "Blessed are the meek, for they shall inherit the earth" is the central beatitude.

1.   It is central because Christ inherits the earth, and He placed a considerable emphasis on meekness during His ministry.

2.   This beatitude is also centrally located in the Beatitudes.

a. Having mourned for our sin, having been emptied of ourselves, and having experienced transformation, we can handle difficult people without irritation.

b. Jesus first modeled this by showing us His grace.

3. Christians understand that the heavenly Father sovereignly superintends difficult and irritating circumstances.

a. We can therefore bow to Him in every circumstance.

b. We can have a spirit of meekness because we know He will work everything together for our good.

4. Jesus draws attention to meekness as an aspect of His own character.

a. He appeals to it as the grounds on which we should come to Him (Matt. 11:28–30).

b. When the Beatitudes are true of us, people should think that they could come to us in order to be shown the way to Christ.

STUDY QUESTIONS

1. Christ came to deal with our guilt and _____ .
    a. Temptation
    b. Hardships
    c. Bondage
    d. Trials

2. The Sermon on the Mount should be understood as a course in advanced Christian living.
    a. True
    b. False

3. The Beatitudes are all original sayings of the Lord Jesus Christ.
    a. True
    b. False

4. In the Gospel narratives, Peter primarily struggles with _____ , a dimension of the Christian life.
    a. Faith
    b. Peace
    c. Suffering
    d. Assurance

5. The only personal characteristics that Christ draws attention to are His meekness and _____ .
    a. Trustworthiness
    b. Graciousness
    c. Loveliness
    d. Lowliness

6. The resurrection of Jesus Christ most directly points to our relationship with the God of _____ .
    a. Purity
    b. Mercy
    c. Peace
    d. Love

DISCUSSION QUESTIONS

1. How are the values of the world radically reversed in the Beatitudes?

2. How are the characteristics described in the Beatitudes the natural outworking of our conversion?

3. How are the Beatitudes exemplified in Jesus Christ?

4. Christ appealed to His own meekness as the grounds on which we should come to Him. What should our own meekness encourage others to do?

3

The Fulfillment of the Law

INTRODUCTION

Jesus Christ came to fulfill the law of God and enable us to keep it. In this lesson, Dr. Ferguson covers the ways in which Jesus has fulfilled the law and the ways in which He taught His disciples to live by it.

LESSON OBJECTIVES

1. To introduce the role of the law of God in the life of the believer
2. To explain the manifold ways Jesus has fulfilled the law

SCRIPTURE READING

That law has but a shadow of the good things to come instead of the true realities.

—Hebrews 10:1a

LECTURE OUTLINE

A. Jesus begins to address the law of God in Matthew 5:17–20.

1. Jesus understands that at this point in the Sermon on the Mount, people are beginning to question why He has yet to mention the law.
   a. It is important to remember that the people who were listening to Jesus lived under the law God gave them through Moses.
   b. People could calculate everything that was happening in Jerusalem by the law, as it regulated people's days, years, and sacrifices.
2. Over time, people began to believe that to be truly spiritual, they needed to go further than God's law.
   a. More than three hundred additional regulations were created by the Pharisees to ensure that the law was kept, and these regulations in turn became regarded as divine laws.

        b.   This is an error that has sometimes been made by Christians.

   3.   The Beatitudes naturally led people to question why Jesus had yet to speak about the law of God.

        a.   The blessedness of the very first psalm is the blessedness of the man who meditates on the law of God day and night (Ps. 1:2).

   4.   Jesus had not yet said anything about the law because He understood that whereas the law can tell us how to live, it cannot empower us to live.

        a.   The law can tell us what to do, but the law does not have the power to enable us to do it.

        b.   Paul learned from Jesus that the gospel gives us the power to fulfill the law and to make the law our delight (Rom. 8:3–4.)

B.   Jesus enumerates several points about the relationship between the Christian and the law of God.

   1.   The law plays an ongoing role in the life of a Christian.

        a.   Christ did not come to destroy the law but to fulfill it.

        b.   Christ embodies the law, and in Him, we see the life to which the law of God points.

   2.   The law functions as a litmus test to measure faithfulness in teaching and the proper estimation of Christian discipleship.

        a.   We cannot jettison the law on the basis that we are New Testament Christians, and in fact, Jesus warns us against such an idea.

        b.   We can evaluate a teacher's estimation of Christian discipleship by his faithfulness to the law.

   3.   The law requires a righteousness that exceeds that of the scribes and Pharisees.

        a.   This was shocking to those listening because the Pharisees were already considered righteous, and Jesus was teaching that His followers need to fulfill the law in ways that the Pharisees could not.

        b.   The Pharisees approached the law in such a way that it could never produce the fullness of the law in their lives; only the gospel can produce such fulfillment.

        c.   Even today, when Moses is read, there remains a veil (2 Cor. 3:15), as Christ is the One to whom the first psalm pointed and who fulfills the promises of the Old Testament.

   4.   The law cannot be fulfilled in our lives if undertaken in our own strength.

        a.   Christians understand that the kingdom of God has broken in and given us new affections that empower us in new ways.

C.   Jesus is also emphasizing that He has come to fulfill the law.

   1.   The law was given to Moses at Sinai as a negative expression (what we are not to do) of the law that had been written in a positive manner (what we are to do) in Adam's heart as the image of God.

      a. Adam functioned instinctively in a way that conformed to the real purpose of the law of God before the fall, and the patriarchs lived in such a way that they did not conform to the law as it was written on their hearts.

2. God published the law on tablets of stone in a largely negative form because His people are spiritually children.
      a. Sometimes the easiest way to teach children is to tell them what not to do, and in order to keep us safe, God expresses most of the Ten Commandments in negative form.
      b. Although they are negative, they still contain the summons of God's original purposes.

3. Jesus fulfilled the moral law of God.
      a. Jesus came to obey where we have disobeyed and to bear the punishment for our disobedience.
      b. Jesus cleanses our hearts and sets us free from our bondage and guilt.

4. Jesus fulfilled the ceremonial law of God.
      a. The law not only contained moral commandments but also contained regulations as to what must be done when a commandment was broken.
      b. Sacrifices were required and functioned as a picture of the gospel, for they reminded the people of their need for forgiveness from God.
      c. The author of Hebrews argues that since the sacrifices had to be repeated, they could not have been the sacrifices that truly took away sin.
      d. Jesus comes to fulfill all the Old Testament pictures that pointed to the forgiveness of sins by the once-for-all sacrifice of a high priest after the order of Melchizedek.
      e. The early church understood that Jesus fulfilled the law and thus laid aside needless sacrifices and rituals.

5. Jesus fulfilled the civil law of God.
      a. The law was given through Moses to a particular nation in order to preserve the promise that the Messiah would come.
      b. The moral law as applied to the civic life of the nation was never meant to be permanent, just as the sacrificial system was never meant to be permanent.
      c. The particular applications of the law to a particular society ended when Jesus became the King of an international society.
      d. The feasts and sacrifices that were held only in Jerusalem are no longer necessary, and thus Christianity goes beyond any one nation.
      e. Jesus' healing of the paralyzed man is a close picture to what Jesus has done: when Jesus rose again, He stood up and rolled away the particular applications of the law of Moses.
      f. The Westminster Confession of Faith teaches that societies can learn many things about justice and equity from how God's law was once applied, yet the emphasis in what Jesus is teaching here is that the Christian life can be lived anywhere.

g. Jesus came in order that the Christian life would be an international reality.

6. Jesus shows how the law of God operates in the life of the Christian.

a. The rest of Matthew 5 concerns the righteousness that runs deeper than that of the scribes and Pharisees.

b. Jesus enables us to keep the law at a deeper level, because the obedience He grants arises from the heart and God has become our Father (Jer. 31:33).

STUDY QUESTIONS

1. True spirituality entails achieving further fulfillment of the law than God requires.

a. True

b. False

2. We can understand the blessedness and priority of the law for the Christian life by looking at the _____ .

a. Psalms

b. Beatitudes

c. Proverbs

d. None of the above

3. Knowing what the law requires is the key that enables you to keep it.

a. True

b. False

4. The _____ law was not given for a particular time and to a particular nation.

a. Civil

b. Moral

c. Ceremonial

d. All of the above

5. Jesus fulfilled the _____ aspect of the law.

a. Civil

b. Moral

c. Ceremonial

d. All of the above

6. The _____ teaches that the application of the moral law to the civic life of Israel can still teach Christians about justice and equity.

a. Westminster Confession of Faith

b. Heidelberg Catechism

c. Thirty-Nine Articles

d. Belgic Confession

DISCUSSION QUESTIONS

1. How is the law a spiritual litmus test for examining someone's teaching?

2. How does a Christian's righteousness exceed that of the scribes and Pharisees?

3. In what ways has Christ fulfilled the law?

4. What does the laying aside of Old Testament sacrifices and rituals by the early church teach us?

4

The Meaning of the Law

INTRODUCTION

The scribes and Pharisees attempted to make God's law easier by adding to it. In this lesson, Dr. Ferguson explains how Christ corrected their misinterpretations of God's law and emphasized the Christian life as one shaped by reconciliation and the gospel.

LESSON OBJECTIVES

1. To emphasize the Christian's identity as salt and light
2. To teach Christ's perfect understanding of the law
3. To show how Christ enables us to keep the law

SCRIPTURE READING

But thanks be to God, that you who were once slaves to sin have become obedient from the heart.

—Romans 6:17a

LECTURE OUTLINE

A. The Christian life is a countercultural life—we are the salt of the earth and the light of the world.

   1. Jesus transforms the lives of His people in such a way that they create a different culture.

   2. Jesus announces who we are in the Beatitudes and likewise announces who we are in declaring us salt and light.

      a. Jesus is not saying, "Do these things in order to become salt and light," but rather, "You are salt and light."

   3. Salt and light function in society in two different ways.

      a. Salt is a preserving agent, so Christians preserve society.

      b. Salt makes you thirsty, so the saltiness of Christians makes others thirsty for what they have in Christ.

   c. Light exposes darkness, so Christians, merely by the way they live their lives, make others conscious that they are sinners.

   d. Light exposes the hearts of people, so just as Christ met opposition in His life, when we speak about or demonstrate Him to others we meet the same opposition.

   e. When believers live as light, they provide not only a standard, but also a direction.

4. Jesus is fulfilling in us the picture of how we were meant to live.

   a. This underlines His statement that He has come fulfill the law, not to destroy it.

B. Jesus teaches how we are to understand the law of God throughout the rest of Matthew 5.

1. During the seventeenth century, there was considerable discussion about the role of the law.

   a. The question was whether to receive the law from the hands of Moses or from the hands of Christ.

   b. The truth is that Moses has no power to enable us to keep the law.

2. John Bunyan's *The Pilgrim's Progress* illustrates the truth that the law, as given to Moses, does not enable us to keep it.

   a. In the narrative, one of Christian's companions is being beaten to death, and he cries out, "Have mercy on me!"

   b. The person beating him then says, "I do not know how to show mercy."

   c. Someone with scars on his hands comes to his rescue.

   d. Christian explains to his companion that the man who was beating him was Moses and the man who rescued him was Christ.

   e. The law drives us to Christ in order to be saved by Him, and then Christ gives us the law to teach us how we should live now that we are saved.

3. Christ is teaching His disciples how the scribes and Pharisees handle the law.

   a. Throughout the rest of Matthew 5, everything Jesus teaches begins with the phrase, "You have heard that it was said . . . " in order to set up a contrast with His teaching.

   b. Jesus is not contradicting the law, because Jesus has already said that His purpose was not to destroy the law.

   c. The usual introduction when the Old Testament is quoted in the New Testament is "God has said . . . " or "It is written . . . ."

   d. When Jesus begins His statements with "You have heard it said . . . ," He is saying that the law had been misinterpreted and that He is teaching about the true inward meaning of the law.

   e. Jesus understands that His hearers have been raised in a community surrounded by rabbinic interpretation and has to teach them how to properly interpret the law.

   f. Jesus does not reference any rabbinic interpretation for what He is saying, and this is why at the end of His sermon people recognize an authority that is unlike that of the scribes and Pharisees.

C. Jesus is reaching into God's law, and He is bringing out of God's law its deeper inner significance.
    1. God gave the law at Sinai in largely negative terms, but it contains positive exhortations as to how God's people are to live.
        a. Jesus is drawing out those positive encouragements here in the Sermon on the Mount.
    2. Jesus not only properly interprets the law; He also helps us to keep the law.
        a. That is the mark of a great teacher.
        b. Jesus teaches us how to do that which we are incapable of doing independently.
    3. When studying the Bible, we have a tendency to take God's commands and go elsewhere to figure out how to fulfill them.
        a. We need to ask God to teach us how to do what He commands within the context of the Bible.
        b. This is what Jesus is doing in the Sermon on the Mount.

D. Jesus illustrates how the proper understanding of the law shapes all of life.
    1. Jesus begins by teaching us that there is more than one way to murder someone, so we are called to live a reconciled life.
        a. The motivation of our hearts when we seek to demean someone or tarnish their reputation is to destroy them, even if by the tongue.
        b. Jesus teaches us to live in contrast to that, because when God commands, "You shall not murder," He is addressing the heart.
        c. We are exposing ourselves to the judgment of God whenever we express our hearts by insulting and demeaning our brother.
        d. Since we have been reconciled to God through Christ, we know what it is to live a life centered on reconciliation with others.
    2. Jesus illustrates the importance of living the reconciled life by relating it to our offerings to God.
        a. It is more important to be reconciled to our brother than to present our offerings before God without reconciliation.
        b. The implications of what Jesus is teaching is that we are to go out of our way to seek reconciliation with our brother just as God sent His own Son to die for us.
        c. When the gospel informs our thinking, then we will be moved to pursue relational reconciliation.
    3. Jesus illustrates the importance of reconciliation through our secular relationships.
        a. We are called to seek reconciliation to prevent our relationships from dissolving to the point that matters can only be settled in a civil court.
        b. We are to use all that is in our power to seek reconciliation with someone before it is too late and no longer an option.

4. Jesus shows how we can live faithfully within our marriage bonds.
    a. Jesus teaches how to have a marriage as God intended—lifelong and free from adultery and divorce.
    b. Jesus addresses how the rabbis had twisted the laws concerning divorce to the extent that a man could divorce his wife for doing something shameful.
    c. Jesus forbids divorce, except on grounds of adultery.
    d. He reveals how to have a faithful marriage free from adultery by keeping our eyes and our hands from wandering.
5. Jesus teaches us how to keep our word.
    a. Jesus is not saying that we should refuse to swear any oath.
    b. Jesus is addressing the practice of swearing oaths that would later be broken because of an appeal to what someone swore by.
    c. People believed swearing on the altar or the temple was not nearly as binding as swearing to God.
    d. Christ is teaching us that our word is our bond, so every word we speak should be faithful to the Lord.
6. Jesus teaches that our righteousness must exceed the righteousness of the scribes and Pharisees.
    a. The driving force behind the reinterpretations of the law by the scribes and Pharisees was to make the law attainable.
    b. In actuality, it is Christ's perfect understanding of the law that makes it attainable.
    c. Jesus is seeking to guide us into a purer life in which we have fruitful relationships, a right heart in marriage, and an understanding that every word we speak is before God.

STUDY QUESTIONS

1. The scribes and Pharisees _____ the law.
    a. Misinterpreted
    b. Misapplied
    c. Distorted
    d. All of the above

2. In the Sermon on the Mount, Jesus specifically teaches us that we expose ourselves to the judgment of God when we are _____ our brother.
    a. Conspiring against
    b. Withholding from
    c. Envious of
    d. Angry with

3. The driving force behind the Pharisees' reinterpretation of the law was to make it easier to fulfill.
   a. True
   b. False

4. _____ is the new center of the Christian life.
   a. Relevance
   b. Acceptance
   c. Reconciliation
   d. Politeness

5. Jesus commands us not to take oaths.
   a. True
   b. False

6. In the Sermon on the Mount, Jesus does *not* address _____ as a topic of how the law had been misapplied.
   a. Oaths
   b. Anxiety
   c. Adultery
   d. Divorce

DISCUSSION QUESTIONS

1. How do salt and light serve as an illustration for the Christian in society?

2. What is the significance of Christ introducing His teachings by the phrase "You have heard it said . . . "?

3. How does Christ's teaching about lust enable someone to keep the commandment "You shall not commit adultery"?

4. What does Dr. Ferguson believe needs to be added to our study of Scripture?

5

Living the Reconciled Life

INTRODUCTION

The reconciliation that we have with God through Jesus Christ changes the way we live in the world and in eternity. In this lesson, Dr. Ferguson explains the illustrations that Jesus uses to teach us how to live a life that always points to Him.

LESSON OBJECTIVE

To provide the cultural significance of the illustrations Jesus uses to teach us about the gospel-centered life

SCRIPTURE READING

All this is from God, who through Christ reconciled us to Himself and gave us the ministry of reconciliation.

—2 Corinthians 5:18

LECTURE OUTLINE

A. The purpose of our study of the Sermon of the Mount is so that we may get inside the logic of the gospel.

1. The logic of the gospel is the life of obedience produced by a transformation of the heart.

   a. It is not that we seek to obey the law so that we may eventually be counted righteous in God's sight; we are already counted righteous, and that motivates us to obey the law.

   b. It is not that we strive for the kingdom of God; once we enter into the kingdom, the power of the kingdom is released in our lives.

   c. We then become salt and light and discover what has been alien to us: we love and fulfill God's law.

    2. The gospel teaches us that grace creates a real love for and obedience to the law.

        a. An illustration of this is how only Christians can truly know and enjoy the privilege of the Lord's Day.

B. Jesus now addresses a well-known statement from the Old Testament in the Sermon on the Mount: "An eye for an eye and a tooth for a tooth" (Lev. 24:20).

    1. This statement is consistently misapplied to personal relationships.

    2. This statement is intended to provide a principle of justice, so that a punishment fits a crime.

        a. It places a limitation on revenge and governs the legal relationships between people.

        b. This principle safeguards society and provides an appropriate legal understanding of a punishment that rightly corresponds to a crime.

    3. Jesus is not teaching that Christians should cease to exercise their legal rights.

        a. The Apostle Paul repeatedly exercised his legal rights as a Roman citizen.

        b. The Bible teaches us that we are to exercise our rights in community.

    4. Jesus is teaching that Christians should not stand on their rights as a first and foremost foundational principle.

        a. People in the United States are incredibly rights driven.

        b. The gospel teaches us to be countercultural, and that if we are in Christ we have offered up all our rights to Him.

    5. Choosing when not to insist upon our rights gives us the opportunity to bear witness to Jesus, who did not even insist on His own rights.

        a. Christ humbled Himself, became obedient to the point of death on the cross, and was exalted by the Father (Phil. 2:5–11).

        b. The paradox is that Christ did not insist on His own rights, but He was given all the rights and privileges as the Son of the Father.

        c. This is to be our mind-set.

C. Jesus uses four illustrations in the Sermon on the Mount to help us understand how we are to bear witness about Him by the way we live.

    1. "Do no resist the one who is evil. But if anyone slaps you on the right cheek, turn to him the other also" (Matt. 5:39).

        a. Jesus is not teaching us to be undiscerning, but he is teaching us a principle.

        b. Jesus particularly mentions the right cheek because a slap on the right cheek would have been a backhanded slap and the grossest of insults.

        c. The principle is that we would allow them to insult and demean us without retaliation, and by doing so we disarm them and give them glimpses of the Lord Jesus Christ.

        d. The great biblical tactic is to let evil exhaust itself until it realizes that it cannot get the best of you.

2. "And if anyone would sue you and take your tunic, let him have your cloak as well" (Matt. 5:40).
   a. In responding to a person of greed, the default reaction of the human heart is not typically one of offering them our possessions.
   b. To be able to freely give of our possessions is beautifully disarming to people who are not Christians.
   c. Jesus draws out an expression of the law that also reveals how much we hold onto our possessions.
   d. The beauty of the gospel can free us from obsessions and enable generosity.

3. "And if anyone forces you to go one mile, go with him two miles" (Matt. 5:41).
   a. Jesus is speaking about denial of personal liberty, because a soldier of a Roman occupying army could conscript an individual for a task. (for example, Simone of Cyrene was conscripted to carry the cross for Jesus).
   b. The limit for conscription by a Roman soldier was one thousand paces, so a willingness to go another one thousand paces for them would be completely disarming to a Roman soldier.
      i. A soldier in this scenario is by definition an enemy: he is a soldier, a Roman soldier, occupying your country, and putting his burden on your back.
      ii. The gospel teaches us to serve our enemies by pointing them to Christ.
   c. This is the same principle that Paul used in his ministry as a servant for Jesus' sake (2 Cor. 4:5), and it is likely that this disposition was the secret of his fruitfulness.

4. "Give to the one who begs from you, and do not refuse the one who would borrow from you" (Matt. 5:42).
   a. Jesus is not teaching us to disregard wisdom and understanding.
   b. Proverbs also teaches us to be wise and discerning with our money.
   c. Jesus is addressing the motivation of the heart.
   d. Sometimes it is too easy for us to look at the passages in Scriptures about wisdom and money as an excuse to be ungenerous.
   e. Shouldn't we prefer to risk looking foolish in our generosity even as we try to be wise and discerning?
   f. Jesus is calling us to share what God has given to us, and we are to hold what God has given us with open hands, free from the clinging influences of wealth and possessions, so that we can be truly free.

STUDY QUESTIONS

1. Dr. Ferguson teaches that the Sermon on the Mount is the _____ of the gospel.
   a. Heart
   b. Logic
   c. Meaning
   d. Implication

2. The _____ life is produced by a transformation of the heart.
    a. Obedient
    b. Circumspect
    c. Transcendent
    d. None of the above

3. Jesus teaches that generosity in the Christian life often involves making unwise decisions with money.
    a. True
    b. False

4. "An eye for an eye, a tooth for a tooth" is a standard for personal relationships.
    a. True
    b. False

5. Jesus illustrates the reconciled life through examples in which our personal _____ is required to point to Him.
    a. Dignity
    b. Property
    c. Freedom
    d. All of the above

6. According to Dr. Ferguson, a key to Paul's fruitfulness was his _____ .
    a. Zeal
    b. Ability
    c. Apostleship
    d. Servanthood

DISCUSSION QUESTIONS

1. What does Christ's example teach us about insisting upon our rights on a personal level?

2. How does the gospel change the way we relate to our possessions?

3. Why is renouncing our personal freedom such an effective witness to Christ?

4. How would you correct someone who quotes "An eye for an eye, a tooth for a tooth" as justification for vengeance?

6

Love Your Enemies

INTRODUCTION

We are called to love our enemies in such a way that we point to the love of our Savior. In this lesson, Dr. Ferguson expands on how Jesus has taught us to love our enemies as the children of a generous heavenly Father.

LESSON OBJECTIVES

1. To correct the misinterpretation of the Mosaic law that to love your neighbor means to hate your enemy
2. To explain the goal, motive, and standard of loving your enemies

SCRIPTURE READING

Repay no one evil for evil, but give thought to do what is honorable in the sight of all.

—Romans 12:17

LECTURE OUTLINE

A. Revisiting where the Sermon on the Mount has taken us thus far is important to understand the context of Jesus' teaching at the end of Matthew 5.
   1. Jesus has taught that the kingdom of God has come, and He has displayed the power of the kingdom through His miracles.
   2. Jesus has taught that the gospel transforms the life that people live within the kingdom.
   3. Jesus has taught that blessedness is rooted in a gospel-centered identity.
      a. People often remark that they are blessed, and what they mean by that is that they have been fortunate in this life.
      b. Jesus is teaching about a blessedness that is produced by God's taking hold of our lives and transforming them.
   4. Jesus has taught that the transformed life leads to a life of righteousness that is more profound and impactful than the righteousness of the scribes and Pharisees.

  a. The scribes and Pharisees were intimidating in their religious practice.

  b. Jesus teaches that true righteousness will produce people that are meek and generous.

 5. Jesus has taught the God's law was always meant to be properly used in pointing us to a beautiful life of freedom and joy by addressing how the law had been misused.

B. Jesus now begins to teach further on the misapplication of God's law and the way it had been misinterpreted: "You shall love your neighbor and hate your enemy."

 1. People believed that the natural implication of God's law was that to love your neighbor was to hate your enemy.

  a. The teachers of the law had created a false dichotomy, because hating your enemy is not a logical necessity of loving your neighbor.

 2. Someone may argue that it is biblical to love your neighbor and hate your enemy based on passages in the Psalms or the actions of Elijah.

  a. In these situations, someone like David is not acting in a private capacity but has an understanding of the position God has given him.

  b. David was given the position of the king, and it was appropriate for him to resist the enemies who were attacking the kingdom.

  c. Jesus is teaching that it is a mistake to apply the principle of resisting your enemy, as it relates to a king and his kingdom, to your personal life.

 3. Jesus wants to teach us further what the Scripture says about the identity of our neighbors.

  a. In Luke's gospel, a lawyer asks Jesus concerning the law, "And who is my neighbor?" (Luke 10:29).

  b. Jesus answers with the parable of the good Samaritan, and He turns the question back on the lawyer, "Which of these three men, do you think, proved to be a neighbor to the man who fell among the robbers?" (Luke 10:36).

  c. The lawyer was seeking to limit his responsibilities, but Jesus showed him that he should be a neighbor to those in need and even to those who turn out to be his enemies.

C. Questions to help us in practical Christian living: What is the goal that is involved?

 1. The goal is to love our neighbors to such an extent that we love even those who have become our enemies.

  a. The idea of falling in love is a romantic experience in which we are overwhelmed with feelings for another.

  b. Jesus teaches us that love is not something that overwhelms and controls us but that it is disposition of the Christian toward others.

  c. The biblical understanding of love is such that we as Christians are determined to give ourselves to others as Christ gave Himself to us.

 2. How do we love our enemies?

     a. It is one thing to know that we are supposed to love our enemies, but it is another thing to know how to do it.

     b. Jesus teaches us how to love our enemies: "Love your enemies and pray for those that persecute you" (Matt. 5:44).

3. We love our enemies by first praying for them.

     a. The moment you begin to pray for your enemies, you can no longer treat them the way you naturally would because it makes you active in your relationship, not defensive.

     b. Praying for our enemies makes us conscious that they are not as intimidating and as in control as we thought they were.

     c. God is in control, and so we pray that God would intervene in their impoverished lives that are full of anger and hatred.

     d. We begin to see them in a different light and even pity their situation because they do not understand the nature of their situation.

     e. Our enemies will come to realize that we are not as small as we seemed, and likewise that they are not as big as they seemed, because we serve a great God.

     f. We focus more on the needs of our enemies and less on our weakness when we pray for them.

     g. This is exactly what Jesus did on the cross: "Father, forgive them, for they know not what they do" (Luke 23:34).

D. Questions to help us in practical Christian living: What is the motive that is involved?

1. Jesus teaches why we are to love our enemies: "Love your enemies and pray for those who persecute you, so that you may be sons of your Father who is in heaven" (Matt. 5:44–45).

     a. Jesus is setting up the implications of what it is to be children of the heavenly Father.

2. "For he makes his sun to rise on the evil and on the good, and sends rain on the just and on the unjust" (Matt. 5:45).

     a. Jesus is showing us that we are children of a generous heavenly Father.

3. "For if you love those who love you, what reward do you have? Do not even the tax collectors do the same?" (Matt. 5:46).

     a. Christ died for us while we were still sinners (Rom. 5:8).

     b. If we love only those who love us, then we are no different from the tax collectors who merely show honor among thieves.

4. The gospel gives us the motive to love our enemies.

     a. Just as the Queen of England once said, "Royal children, royal manners," so we are to show that we are God's children.

     b. We can ask the Lord to help us to be like Him with respect to our enemies.

5. We will begin to see our enemies as desperately needy people.

a. If we see ourselves as royal children of the heavenly Father who share in His wonderful generosity, we will become more generous to others.

b. We can afford to be generous to our enemies in such a way that our generosity disarms them.

E. Questions to help us in practical Christian living: What is the standard that is involved?

1. Jesus teaches the standard by which we are to love our enemies: "You therefore must be perfect, as your heavenly Father is perfect" (Matt. 5:48).

2. The word translated "perfect" is the same word that is elsewhere translated in the New Testament as "mature."

   a. Jesus is teaching us that we should be grown up in our generosity.

3. The heavenly Father, who has displayed His perfection in the generosity He has shown to His enemies, is our standard for generosity.

4. Robert Murray M'Cheyne wrote by way of prayer, "Make me as holy as a saved sinner can be."

   a. Just as in this prayer, we are to model the heavenly Father, so that people can see the resemblance, especially in the way we love our enemies.

STUDY QUESTIONS

1. The Pharisees believed that if we are commanded to love our neighbors it is illogical to hate our enemies.
   a. True
   b. False

2. Theologians suggest that we determine the _____ of a teaching to help us in our practical Christian living.
   a. Goal
   b. Motive
   c. Standard
   d. All of the above

3. _____ is a central element to extending love to our enemies.
   a. Conversation
   b. Confession
   c. Openness
   d. Prayer

4. God's _____ makes our enemies appear smaller than we originally thought.
   a. Aseity
   b. Eternality
   c. Sovereignty
   d. Transcendence

5. "Royal children, royal manners" is an expression that was originally used as an example of the goal of Christ's teaching.
    a. True
    b. False

6. Loving our enemies with the Father's _____ will showcase that we are His children.
    a. Standard
    b. Perfection
    c. Generosity
    d. All of the above

DISCUSSION QUESTIONS

1. Why do the prayers of David not support an argument for hating our enemies?

2. What was the lawyer trying to accomplish by asking Jesus, "Who is my neighbor?"

3. How does Christian love differ in meaning from the love described in the common expression "I fell in love"?

4. How does prayer change our relationship with our enemies?

7

Scribes, Pharisees, Hypocrites

INTRODUCTION

Disciples of the Lord Jesus Christ live in marked contrast from the Pharisees, as true righteousness is for God's glory, not our own. In this lesson, Dr. Ferguson develops on how knowing God as Father is the essential remedy for pharisaical hypocrisy.

LESSON OBJECTIVES

1. To expose the religious hypocrisy of the scribes and Pharisees
2. To describe how the knowledge of God as Father was perfectly revealed in Jesus Christ and how it changes the motivations of our hearts

SCRIPTURE READING

Truly, I say to you, they have received their reward.

—Matthew 6:16b

For where your treasure is, there your heart will be also.

—Matthew 6:21

LECTURE OUTLINE

A. There is an inner logic to the Sermon on the Mount and the whole of Jesus' ministry.
  1. Jesus has come to establish the kingdom of God.
     a. He was publicly appointed as the King at His baptism (Ps. 2:7).
  2. Jesus has come to do battle with Satan who has stolen the world from humanity in order to destroy it.
     a. Jesus is the first individual in history to withstand the assaults of the evil one.

   b. Satan retreated from tempting Jesus in the wilderness for a more oppor-
       tune time, and Jesus continues to proclaim the kingdom.
3. Jesus also displays the power of the kingdom through signs and wonders, restor-
    ing men and women to the physical life that God intended for them—the blind
    see, the lame walk, lepers are cleansed, and the deaf hear.
4. Jesus teaches His disciples that the power of the kingdom not only restores and
    transforms human bodies but also restores and transforms human lives.
    a. There are blessings in Jesus Christ that fundamentally change what we
        are.
5. The entirety of Matthew 5 can be summed up by the word *fulfillment*.
    a. The Beatitudes are the fulfillment of the Old Testament promises of what
        the transformed life would look like.
    b. Christ fulfills the law of God and enables His disciples to keep the law in a
        deeper way than the scribes and Pharisees.

B. Jesus now focuses on the way that the scribes and Pharisees practice religion and
    how His disciples are to live in contrast to it.
1. Jesus highlights three leading elements in the religious life of the Pharisees.
    a. These are the same elements that are on display in the parable about the
        tax collector and the Pharisee (Luke 18:9–14).
    b. The Pharisee is praying, boasting about his mercy ministry, and empha-
        sizing his rigorous discipline.
2. Jesus addresses the way Pharisees give alms, pray, and fast so that all can see.
3. Jesus preaches with a consistent rhythm and pattern of speech in these three
    sections of the Sermon on the Mount.
4. He stresses three main points: the motivation in our discipleship, the result of
    our discipleship, and the potential losses that could result from our discipleship.
5. Jesus speaks about the motivation in our discipleship and the nature of
    hypocrisy.
    a. *Hypocrite* comes from the Greek and referred to an actor who would put
        on a mask in order to change characters.
    b. A hypocrite does things in order to maintain appearances.
    c. Jesus deals with properly understanding our discipleship in contrast with
        religious activity done for the sake of being seen by others.
6. Jesus speaks about the reward of such discipleship.
    a. Jesus teaches that those who do their good works in order to be seen have
        no reward from the heavenly Father.
    b. Jesus shows what hypocrites actually look like to God by giving anecdotes
        such as sounding a trumpet before giving to the poor.
    c. Jesus points out how the Pharisees pray and fast in order to be seen.
7. Jesus is not being malicious.
    a. Jesus wants to reveal how God views them.
    b. Jesus is exposing the problem of having no reward with the Father.

c. Jesus is teaching that living in the presence of God in relationship to Him as Father is the solution.

C. Knowing God as Father is fully revealed through Christ and is the essential remedy for hypocrisy.

  1. God is referred to as "Father" ten times in the first eighteen verses of Matthew 6.
     a. There is not a group of eighteen verses, eighteen chapters, or eighteen books in the Old Testament that refer to God personally as "Father" ten times.
     b. Neither does the entire Old Testament contain ten intimate references to God as "Father."

  2. The references to God as "Father" in the Old Testament tend to fit two categories.
     a. They reference God as creator of the universe.
     b. They reference God as creator of Israel.
     c. Exceptions to this categorization: the king in relationship to God as a son and the metaphors used describing the qualities of God.

  3. There is not a reference to God as "Father" in the Old Testament in the same way that Jesus speaks of how we are to understand God as "Father."
     a. God finally and fully reveals Himself in Jesus Christ.
     b. It is only when the Son is revealed that the Trinity is understood.
     c. If Jesus is the Son, then the first person of the Trinity must be Father.

  4. Now that the Son has come we begin to know God in such a way that it changes our chief concerns.
     a. We become more concerned with what the Father thinks of us than what other people think of us.
     b. This changes the way we practice our righteousness.

  5. The way we give will be different.
     a. We give because we love the Father and want to share the Father's heart for the needy.
     b. We are not giving to benefit ourselves but want to extend the riches the Father has given us to others.
     c. Whether someone notices is irrelevant because we are doing it for the Father.

  6. "They have their reward in full" is an expression commonly found on ancient receipts that is similar to the expression "paid in full."
     a. If you want the praise of men, that is what you will get, but you will have no reward from the heavenly Father.

  7. We cannot truly earn a reward from a heavenly Father who gives freely.
     a. As a good earthly father does, He gives us more than we are owed.
     b. In our giving and through our spiritual disciplines, we are not concerned with what the left or right hand is doing.
     c. We want to respond to the Father's invitation to seek His face, and when we have been in His presence, our face begins to reflect His.

d. A hymn of Anna Letitia Waring prompts us to pray for "a heart at leisure from itself to soothe and sympathize"; it is this that we discover when we come to know God as Father.

STUDY QUESTIONS

1. *Fulfillment* is the one-word description of Matthew 6.
    a. True
    b. False

2. The parable of the tax collector and the Pharisee in Luke 18 highlights _____ as the focal point of the religion of the Pharisees.
    a. Acts of mercy
    b. Prayer
    c. Fasting
    d. All of the above

3. The Pharisees intended their religious practice to draw attention to their _____ .
    a. Love
    b. Mercy
    c. Discipline
    d. Hypocrisy

4. Jesus contrasts the Pharisees' hypocrisy with the _____ of discipleship.
    a. Results
    b. Motivations
    c. Potential losses
    d. All of the above

5. "They have their reward" is a phrase found on ancient versions of what we would today call receipts.
    a. True
    b. False

6. Old Testament references to God as Father describe His relationship to _____ .
    a. Israel
    b. Kings
    c. Creation
    d. All of the above

DISCUSSION QUESTIONS

1. Where does the word *hypocrite* come from? How does it accurately describe the Pharisees?

2. What is significant about the references to God as Father in Matthew 6?

3. How did Jesus Christ, the Son of God, deepen our relationship with and knowledge of God?

4. What is a Christian's primary motivation for giving to the needy?

8

Knowing God
as Father

INTRODUCTION

The essence of knowing God as Father manifests itself in prayer through our identity in Jesus Christ. In this lesson, Dr. Ferguson introduces the Lord's Prayer by describing how Jesus changes the way we come to our heavenly Father.

LESSON OBJECTIVE

To instruct our attitude and approach in prayer

SCRIPTURE READING

And because you are sons, God has sent the Spirit of his Son into our hearts, crying, "Abba! Father!"

—Galatians 4:6

LECTURE OUTLINE

A. Jesus is teaching us that we can never know ourselves until we know the heavenly Father, and that the essence of knowing the Father manifests itself in prayer.

   1. Jesus has been showing us how hypocrites look in the eyes of the Father because He wants us to know ourselves.

     a. "Know yourself" is a central element in Greek philosophy.

   2. John Calvin opens his *Institutes of the Christian Religion* by emphasizing the importance of the knowledge of God and the knowledge of ourselves.

     a. We cannot come to know ourselves unless we also come to know the Father.

   3. The central section of Matthew 6:1–18 involves prayer.

     a. Hebrew literature is unlike English literature because it places the primary and significant points in the middle and not at the end.

4. Jesus teaches us how to pray.
   a. Jesus is contrasting the right way to pray with hypocritical prayer.
   b. The disciples asked Jesus to teach them to pray in Luke's account of the Lord's Prayer, and in light of John 17, it is no surprise why they inquired.
5. The Lord's Prayer is set within the context of our identity as children of the heavenly Father.
   a. Jesus has introduced us to the Father, and as sons of the Father, we enjoy an inheritance.
   b. Jesus has taught us to pray as members of His family.
6. The fact that we have been named in Christ is woven deep into the theology of the Gospels.
   a. Jesus is baptized symbolically into our sins, which are placed on Him at the cross.
   b. We are then baptized into Him, and a marvelous exchange takes place by which we are renamed and brought into His family.
   c. Baptism is a family naming ceremony, and just like when your parents named you, it did not change you internally, but it has a profound impact on your life.
   d. Being named in Christ gives you an identity that tells you who you are, so now you can pray to the Father just as Jesus prayed to the Father.
7. In Jesus Christ, we can pray, "Abba! Father!"
   a. Even Christians living in a Greek-speaking culture prayed, "Abba! Father!" because they had been introduced to the Father by the Lord Jesus Christ (Rom. 8:15; Gal. 4:6).

B. Jesus teaches us how knowing God as Father influences our attitude in prayer.
   1. Whenever we are exhorted not to do something in the New Testament, there is always a replacement.
      a. If we are told to put something off, we are always told what will take its place.
      b. Thomas Chalmers' sermon *The Expulsive Power of a New Affection* is a perfect example of what the gospel does in replacing our old affections.
      c. Jesus exhorts us not to pray to be seen or to heap up empty phrases to be heard, and then He shows us how to pray.
   2. True prayer directs our eyes to the heavenly Father.
      a. Spurgeon once commented on a newspaper article that described a prayer as the "finest prayer offered to a Boston congregation."
      b. The litmus test of our prayer should be whether our eyes are upon the Father.
      c. We should have an understanding of our glorious access to Him and our security with Him.
      d. This is at the heart of why Jesus teaches us to find private places to pray, and to say, "Our Father."

3. Private prayer does not mean that we are no longer to pray publicly.
   a. Jesus prayed regularly in public.
   b. If prayer were meant to be exclusively private, Jesus would not have told us to customarily pray, "Our Father."
   c. Jesus is teaching us that prayer is primarily a relationship of our heart to the Father.
   d. Prayer is about our attitude and not about the number or eloquence of our words, as if they elicit God's hearing.
4. The heavenly Father knows what we need before we ask Him, but that does not mean we no longer need to pray.
   a. We do not pray in order to tell God what we need or to tell Him things He doesn't know.
   b. We pray to discover how God is moving in our lives and how He is directing us to catch up with His purposes.
   c. God also uses our prayer as a means by which His blessing is distributed to the world.
   d. God does not want to fulfill His purposes without catching us up to them, and this is our great privilege as His children.

C. Jesus teaches us how knowing God as Father influences our approach in prayer.
   1. It is also the fact that God is our King that changes our attitude and serves as the basis for our ability to bring petitions to Him.
      a. It is His identity as Father and King that changes how we pray.
      b. He is a King, and it is our privilege to come before His infinite majesty.
      c. He is infinite majesty and simultaneously our Father, and this changes the way we commune with Him.
   2. The tension of knowing the awesomeness of God and the tenderness of God is indescribable.
      a. It is when we grasp these two things that we are stretched spiritually and feel the delight, glory, and wonder of coming to Him.
      b. He wants to be known by us as a Father who is in heaven and at the same time our heavenly Father.
   3. Many people have difficulties thinking about God as Father because of the relationship to their own father.
      a. We cannot extrapolate from fatherhood of our earthly fathers to the fatherhood of our heavenly Father.
      b. We also cannot take our confidence in God's fatherly care for us by our ability to read the providential circumstances of our lives.
   4. The reason we trust His heavenly fatherhood is because He gave us everything He has in Jesus Christ and in the gift of the Holy Spirit.
      a. This is the same gospel logic that Paul uses to show that God will stop at nothing to bless us (Rom. 8:32).
      b. The cross convinces us of the love of the heavenly Father, and it is through the cross that we are able pray in the name of Jesus Christ.

STUDY QUESTIONS

1. *The Expulsive Power of a New Affection*—a sermon title that accurately describes how the gospel works—was preached by _____ .
    a. John Owen
    b. John Calvin
    c. Thomas Watson
    d. Thomas Chalmers

2. The Sermon on the Mount teaches that we should only pray in private.
    a. True
    b. False

3. Our attitude and our _____ in prayer are what truly matter.
    a. Ability
    b. Amount
    c. Approach
    d. Articulacy

4. Our privilege in prayer is in between the tension of the awesomeness and the _____ of God.
    a. Loftiness
    b. Weightiness
    c. Tenderness
    d. Meekness

5. We gain confidence in the fatherhood of God by examining the providential circumstances in our lives.
    a. True
    b. False

6. The _____ convinces us of the love of the heavenly Father.
    a. Son
    b. Spirit
    c. Cross
    d. All of the above

DISCUSSION QUESTIONS

1. What is the significance of baptism for our relationship with the heavenly Father in prayer?

2. What is the litmus test and aim of our prayers?

3. Why do we pray if the Father knows what we need before we ask Him?

4. How can you help explain the fatherhood of God to someone who has difficulty thinking of God as Father because of his or her earthly father?

9

The Lord's Prayer

INTRODUCTION

The Lord's Prayer is the pattern for prayer and the pattern for life. In this lesson, Dr. Ferguson teaches us how the Lord's Prayer helps us to live in the presence of God so that we would seek His glory and trust Him in all our needs.

LESSON OBJECTIVES

1. To identify the sections of the Lord's Prayer
2. To detail each petition of the Lord's Prayer

SCRIPTURE READING

Therefore let everyone who is godly offer prayer to you at a time when you may be found; surely in a rush of great waters, they shall not reach him.

—Psalm 32:6

LECTURE OUTLINE

A. The Lord's Prayer is a pattern for prayer and a pattern for life.
  1. It is helpful to think of the Lord's Prayer as a pattern for living so that we can learn to live in the presence of God.
      a. The title of the medieval work *The Practice of the Presence of God* teaches us that prayer is not a compartmentalized part of our lives.
      b. Prayer is an overflow from the way we live our lives before the face of God.
  2. Calvin used the Latin phrase *coram Deo* to express how we live in the presence of God, and so we also live in communion with God.
      a. As we grow as Christians, we develop an awareness that we are living in two different worlds.
      b. The broader consideration is that we are living in God's world, in the company of the Father.

      c. Jesus' life was characterized by an understanding of God's presence.

      d. He taught His disciples to pray and introduced them to the life that acknowledges the ever-present heavenly Father.

B. The first section of the Lord's Prayer focuses on the glory of God and His name.

    1. Martin Luther's *A Simple Way to Pray* was written to instruct his barber on how to use the Lord's Prayer as an outline for prayer.

      a. One of Luther's great watchwords was "Let God be God."

    2. Letting God be God is what the first petition of the Lord's Prayer focuses our attention on.

      a. We are praying that God would be God to us, that He would come to be seen as God to the world, and that His kingdom would be the fruit of our lives.

    3. We come to God as Father recognizing that He is holy.

      a. We appreciate how wonderful our intimacy with Him is because He is holy.

      b. We understand that His name is holy, so we want to see His name treated as holy.

    4. We are zealous for the Lord's name, and it hurts us when the Lord's name is taken in vain.

      a. When people use the Lord's name in vain, they are talking about our Father.

      b. We are praying that God's name would be recognized as an expression of who God is.

C. The first section of the Lord's Prayer focuses on the glory of God and His kingdom.

    1. We pray, "Your kingdom come," even though the kingdom of God has already come in the person of Christ.

      a. God has always progressively worked in history.

      b. Moses and his people only caught glimpses of Jesus through the sacrifices.

      c. The prophet Isaiah pointed to the Suffering Servant who would deal with Israel's spiritual bondage.

      d. In this sense, Isaiah knew more about Jesus than Moses or Abraham did.

    2. God works exactly the same way as His kingdom is established in Jesus.

      a. Jesus came and defeated the lord of this world, and He wants the kingdom now to move into the world.

      b. Jesus sends His disciples throughout the world because all authority has been given to Him.

      c. Christ's authority has not yet extended into the hearts of all people, and that is what we are praying for.

      d. We want to see the transforming power of God breaking into people's lives.

3. The kingdom is to move from expressing God's majesty in heaven to expressing God's majesty on earth.
   a. We are praying that we would display God's majesty in our own lives among His people.
   b. Jesus commands us to be perfect as our heavenly Father is perfect, and so we pray for the full expression of God's image in our lives.
4. We live in the presence of God so that the obedience to the Father that is displayed in the heavenly court will be displayed in our earthly lives.
   a. Izaak Walton said of Richard Sibbes, "Heaven was in him before he was in heaven."
   b. This is true of every Christian, because by the Holy Spirit we have the love of God in our hearts so that we taste heaven even on this earth.
   c. The more we taste it, the greater is our desire to live with a heavenly atmosphere, so that people will see our good works and glorify God.

D. The second section of the Lord's Prayer focuses on our needs.
   1. God is adequate to answer all of our prayers and supply all of our needs.
      a. We know who God is, so we are able to ask Him for our daily bread.
      b. The Lord's Prayer is not only a pattern for prayer but is also a pattern for our lives, so we begin to think in terms of daily dependence on the Lord.
   2. The abundance in the twenty-first century may cause us to miss the implications of petitioning the Lord for daily bread.
      a. The prayer is intended to spread into the details of our lives because we could not even enjoy the things we mistakenly think are ours if it were not for God's provision and our dependence on Him.
      b. A good example of this is how a medication may work for someone and not another person.
      c. A Christian sees that, like medicine that doesn't work, the resources of this world are in themselves empty, and so they are only satisfying insofar as they are received in dependence upon the God who provides them.
      d. God's provision in turn leads us to live in His presence and in dependent faith.
      e. Jesus teaches us that dependence on the Lord is the only way for our needs truly to be met.
   3. Dependent living changes the way we pray, because when we bring our requests to God, we will ask ourselves, "Do we really need it?"
      a. Prayer delivers us from the clinging nature of materialism.
      b. The realization that we are praying to the King of the universe puts the importance of what we ask for into perspective.
      c. We learn to live without the things we think we need.
      d. Jesus is giving us a simple principle that brings us back to basic simplicities.

E. The second section of the Lord's Prayer focuses on our daily need to forgive.
    1. Jesus further expanded on the Lord's Prayer, "For if you forgive others their trespasses, your heavenly Father will also forgive you."
        a. If we are not engaged in forgiving others, then it is evident that we have not experienced the forgiveness of God.
        b. The forgiveness of God washes away the unforgiveness of our soul.
    2. This does not mean that we are asking God to forgive us because we forgive others, as if to say, "If I forgive them, then you should forgive me."
        a. God comes to us with hands full of forgiveness, and as we look at and contemplate such forgiveness, our unforgiveness is washed away.
    3. We are to ask for forgiveness even though we are justified.
        a. Here in the Lord's Prayer and throughout the New Testament, we are commanded and encouraged to ask forgiveness.
        b. Justification means that our sins are pardoned and we are counted righteous in God's sight.
        c. God is not only the Judge who justifies, but also the heavenly Father who has entered into relationship with us.
    4. The Judge who becomes our Father is an illustration of justification, adoption, and the reason why we ask for forgiveness.
        a. The Judge once and for all acquits us, but we live with the Father forever.
        b. We do not want to grieve Him, so when we do, we seek forgiveness.
        c. We live in a sensitive love for the heavenly Father so that we will never grieve or offend Him.
    5. This is what the Bible means when it speaks about the fear of God.
        a. The fear of God is not cringing terror.
        b. The fear of God is the spirit in a child of God that wants to see the Father smile on their life and avoid anything that would welcome a frown.
    6. We need to come to God when we grieve Him.
        a. We still have an instinct to hide from God when we grieve Him.
        b. When we remember that He is our heavenly Father, we go to Him, and we find His fatherly embrace and forgiveness.

F. The second section of the Lord's Prayer focuses on our need to be delivered from temptation.
    1. Our need for forgiveness leads us to pray to be delivered from temptation.
    2. God does not lead us into temptation, but Jesus was led into temptation.
        a. In God's wisdom, He may expose us to testing in order that we may resist and grow stronger.
    3. It is not always the case that sinful desire and opportunity are present.
        a. When external opportunity and internal desire are present, we stand in what the New Testament refers to as "the evil day" (Eph. 6:13).
        b. We then need to put on the full armor of God.

4. Sometimes the heavenly Father wants to show us that we trust Him.
   a. He wants to show us that He is able to keep us from falling and show us that our trust in Him is real.
   b. It is a fearful thought that we might fail in moments of temptation, so we pray in dependence on the Father.
5. Because the Father truly cares about us, He provides for us, forgives us, keeps us, and protects us.

STUDY QUESTIONS

1. The Lord's Prayer is divided into _____ sections.
   a. Two
   b. Three
   c. Four
   d. None of the above

2. *Coram Deo* was a favorite expression of _____ .
   a. Thomas Watson
   b. Richard Sibbes
   c. Martin Luther
   d. John Calvin

3. "Let God be God" was a favorite expression of _____ .
   a. Thomas Watson
   b. Richard Sibbes
   c. Martin Luther
   d. John Calvin

4. The fear of God is the spirit in a child of God that wants to see the Father's smile.
   a. True
   b. False

5. Our _____ is a primary reason why we ask for forgiveness from our heavenly Father.
   a. Justification
   b. Sanctification
   c. Glorification
   d. Adoption

6. Prayer and the _____ are our greatest allies when external opportunity meets internal desire in our temptations.
   a. Heavenly Father
   b. Armor of God
   c. Holy Spirit
   d. All of the above

DISCUSSION QUESTIONS

1. Why is it important to think of the Lord's Prayer not only as a pattern for praying but also as a pattern for living?

2. Why do we pray, "Your kingdom come," if the kingdom has already come in the person of Jesus Christ?

3. How and why does the Lord's Prayer change what we ask for?

4. If we have already been forgiven, why does Jesus give us a model prayer in which we must ask forgiveness?

10

The Cure
For Our Anxiety

INTRODUCTION

Our understanding of God, or the lack thereof, can either be the cause or the cure for our anxiety. In this lesson, Dr. Ferguson expands on the illustrations that Jesus uses to teach about the gospel cure for our anxiety—knowing our Father.

LESSON OBJECTIVE

To identify the causes and cure for all our anxieties

SCRIPTURE READING

Therefore do not be anxious, saying, "What shall we eat?" or "What shall we drink?" or "What shall we wear?" For the Gentiles seek after all these things, and your heavenly Father knows that you need them all.

—Matthew 6:32–33

LECTURE OUTLINE

A. So far in our study of the Sermon on the Mount, there is a foundation and pattern to Jesus' teaching.

    1. He is the King in God's kingdom, and the kingdom has come.

        a. He has shown the power of the kingdom and is now teaching people about kingdom discipleship.

    2. The chapters of the Sermon on the Mount can be summed up in one word: Matthew 5 with *fulfillment* and Matthew 6 with *Father*.

        a. In Matthew 6:1–18, Jesus teaches us how the knowledge of God as heavenly Father delivers us from hypocrisy.

b. In Matthew 6:19–34, Jesus teaches us that the knowledge of God as heavenly Father delivers us from anxiety.

B. *Therefore* is a key word to pay attention to in this section of the Sermon on the Mount.

1. If hypocrisy is a plague among religious people, then anxiety is an almost universal plague in the Western world.
    a. Jesus takes great care and concern about religious hypocrisy, but He also has a great tenderness towards us as anxious people.

2. Jesus knows that we want to deal with our anxiety.
    a. If our anxiety is not caused by a chemical disorder in our bodies, then putting chemicals into our bodies will not cure it.

3. Jesus uses the word *therefore* to link together Matthew 6:10–24 and 6:25–34.
    a. *Therefore* is an important word in the Bible.
    b. A primary example is how Paul uses it to teach the application of the gospel to the Christian life in Romans 12.
    c. Paul, in referring back to what he had already said, does exactly what Jesus does in the Sermon on the Mount.
    d. Jesus is showing us that what He is teaching on before speaking about anxiety is directly tied to the cure for our anxiety.

4. "Therefore" signals that Jesus is pointing out the causes for our anxiety.
    a. He diagnoses the causes of our anxiety like a physician would diagnose our physical ailments.
    b. Jesus diagnoses the symptoms of our anxiety before pointing out the deeper problem of our anxiety.

C. Where we place our treasures, the light from which we see, and the masters that we serve all create anxiety.

1. Our possessions create anxiety.
    a. It is important to point out that Jesus is making a distinction between our possessions and our treasures.
    b. Jesus understands that possessions are legitimate, but we are not to view them as ultimate.
    c. If we view our possessions as ultimate, we have replaced the real nature of lasting treasure with a recipe for anxiety.
    d. The more we have and the more insurance we need, the more anxious we get.
    e. We create anxiety because our treasure is in the wrong storehouse.

2. We create anxiety by seeing only darkness.
    a. When we do not see things in the proper light, we do not know where to find lasting treasure.
    b. If our eyes are focused on things of passing value then we are going to be full of darkness.
    c. Looking for lasting treasure where it cannot be found is a recipe for anxiety.

3. Attempting to serve two masters creates anxiety.
   a. Jesus started these illustrations by focusing on materialism and like an expert physician moves to the motivations of the heart.
   b. The world competes with the gospel for our hearts, and when the blessings God gives us become our master, there will be anxiety.
   c. This is a great struggle for many people who are being called into Christ's kingdom because they realize the cost of true discipleship.
   d. When we serve two masters, we discover that the blessings that were intended to be our servants now rule over us.
   e. The promise that we will gain a hundredfold of what we leave behind for the sake of Christ can only be fulfilled when those things are no longer our masters and are enjoyed the way they were meant to be.

D. Not thinking clearly about the gospel produces anxiety because the gospel provides the cure for our anxiety.
   1. "Therefore" marks Jesus' transition from describing the symptoms of our anxiety to providing its cure.
   2. Christians need to think about the implications of the Father's reign in this world.
      a. We need to be delivered from what would appear to any outsider as the evident gods of this world—what we eat, what we drink, what we wear.
      b. The only way we can be delivered from these is if we understand that they are bad masters and that the heavenly Father is the best of all possible masters.
   3. We have no need to be anxious because the Father shows us what a great provider He is through the way He provides for all His creatures.
      a. The Father provides for the birds of the air and dresses the flowers in the field.
   4. Jesus identifies those who live as if the Father did not reign in this world with pagans, Gentiles, and unbelievers.
      a. If we profess to be Christ's disciples, we are not to think and live like pagans.
      b. Jesus is calling us to yield our entire life to Him.
   5. Seeking first the kingdom of God allows us not to be anxious about tomorrow.
      a. We have to throw ourselves into the hands of the Father.

STUDY QUESTIONS

1. Jesus teaches us about anxiety in the section of the Sermon on the Mount that is summarized by the word _____ .
   a. Transformation
   b. Fulfillment
   c. Judgment
   d. Father

2. Jesus doesn't distinguish between our possessions and our treasures.
    a. True
    b. False

3. Anxiety caused by an obsession with what we will drink, what we will eat, and what we will wear identifies us with _____ .
    a. Pagans
    b. Gentiles
    c. Unbelievers
    d. All of the above

4. Jesus can be compared to a _____ in His assessment of our need to know God as Father.
    a. Farmer
    b. Lawyer
    c. Physician
    d. Fisherman

5. Our _____ have the potential to cause anxiety in the Christian life.
    a. Masters
    b. Possessions
    c. Priorities
    d. All of the above

6. Anxiety is a plague among religious people as hypocrisy is a plague in the Western world.
    a. True
    b. False

DISCUSSION QUESTIONS

1. When studying your Bible, to what should the word *therefore* alert you?

2. What should be the Christian's attitude toward material possessions?

3. How does Jesus move climatically through the causes of our anxiety?

4. Which of the causes of our anxiety do you struggle with most? How does the Sermon on the Mount apply to your specific anxiety?

11

Condemnation and Discernment

INTRODUCTION

"Judge not, that you be not judged" is the most misunderstood teaching from the Sermon on the Mount. In this lesson, Dr. Sinclair Ferguson clarifies what Jesus truly meant within the greater context of applying the wisdom of God to our lives.

LESSON OBJECTIVES

1. To correct the misuse of "judge not, that you be not judged"
2. To warn of the dangers of using judgment as condemnation and not using judgment as discernment
3. To demonstrate how Christians are to apply the wisdom of God

SCRIPTURE READING

Do not judge by appearances, but judge with right judgment.

—John 7:24

Render true judgments, show kindness and mercy to one another.

—Zechariah 7:9

LECTURE OUTLINE

A. *Judgment* summarizes the last chapter of the Sermon on the Mount.

   1. "Judge not, that you be not judged" (Matt. 7:1) are the most misunderstood words in the Sermon on the Mount.

      a. The idea of judgment is the running theme of Matthew 7.

      b. The word *judgment* has nuances of meaning according to the context in which it is used.

      c. Jesus is teaching that judgment is important in the life of the believer.

B. Jesus begins by speaking about judgment as condemnation.

1. People who seek to condemn someone else without the proper evidence condemn themselves.

a. They lay the groundwork for their own condemnation.

b. God will judge them with the measure by which they judge others.

c. If a person does not have the grounds to condemn another person, he is seeking to dismiss and demean the other person.

d. This motivation is the groundwork for God's judgment.

e. Jesus is teaching that we must be very careful in judging others.

2. Jesus uses the parables in Luke 15 as perfect illustrations of judgment that becomes the grounds for condemnation.

a. The parables of the lost sheep, the lost coin, and the prodigal son were all directed to those who judged Jesus for welcoming sinners.

b. Each of the parables moves climatically: a hundred sheep, one is lost; ten coins, one is lost; two sons, one is lost.

c. The elder brother is the climax of these parables, for the elder brother represents the Pharisees whom Jesus was intentionally addressing.

d. Paul addresses this same spirit when writing to the church in Rome how we should not judge our brothers as if we were their masters (Rom. 14:4).

3. Jesus uses animated language to show people what they look like when they judge others.

a. It is comical that the man with the plank of wood sticking out of his eye is worried about the speck of dust in his brother's eye.

b. Jesus is trying to show us what people look like to God when they judge others.

4. Knowing the heavenly Father is the remedy for our judgments as condemnation.

a. The Father had every reason to condemn us for our sins, but instead had mercy on us.

b. The knowledge of the Father's mercy delivers us from condemning others.

C. Jesus teaches us that we must exercise judgment as discernment.

1. Judgment used as discernment is absolutely essential.

a. People who use "judge not" as a defense against Christians have not truly read the Sermon on the Mount.

2. It is important to use discernment in order to know how to talk to someone.

a. This is exactly what Jesus means in saying, "Do not throw your pearls before pigs" (Matt. 7:6).

3. We must exercise discernment to bring the gospel to different situations.

a. We need to be able to discern the way people respond to the gospel.

b. Jesus did this when He allowed the rich young ruler to walk away.

c. Jesus discerned His true spiritual condition of the rich young ruler as unclean, as his being a spiritual "pig."

4. "Answer not a fool according to his folly . . . answer a fool according to his folly" (Prov. 26:4–5) is not a contradiction.
   a. These proverbs show the importance of using spiritual discernment.
   b. There are times when it is important to stand up to the folly of this world and to defend the gospel, and there are times when it is best to remain silent.
   c. It is reckless to evangelize without discernment.
5. Our immediate reaction should be the humble realization that we need the wisdom spoken about in Scripture.
   a. Wisdom needs to be asked for, pursued, and desired (James 1:5).

D. There needs to be judgment in order for us to know how to get wisdom.
   1. Jesus teaches us, "Ask, and it will be given you; seek, and you will find; knock, and will be opened for you" (Matt. 7:7).
      a. Wisdom comes from increasing our knowledge of God and our ability to apply it to every situation.
   2. We can be sure that if our heavenly Father will give us wisdom if we ask Him for it.
      a. Even evil men know how to give good gifts to their children, so how much more a good God?
   3. The Father wants us to have wisdom in order to be able to negotiate in a world that is often hostile to Him and to those who love Him.
      a. We get this wisdom from the Word and from the Spirit to help us understand what God has to say about our situations.
   4. This wisdom is especially needed for the areas God's Word does not directly address.
      a. For example, we must apply the wisdom of God to our lives in order to know whom to marry or where to live.
      b. Jesus teaches us that this type of wisdom will be ours if we only ask the Father.

E. "So whatever you wish that others do to you, do also for them, for this is the Law and the Prophets."
   1. The Golden Rule is situated perfectly in context.
      a. We are not to condemn others, but we are to practice spiritual discernment.
      b. In order to practice spiritual discernment, we need to grow in wisdom and understanding.
      c. We then need the principles to help us discern God's purposes for situations where the Bible does not directly speak.
   2. The Golden Rule shows how the general teaching of Scripture can be applied to specific situations.
      a. The Golden Rule and the *Shema* help us to exercise the wisdom of God.
      b. The Golden Rule is a general principle to apply when the Bible does not speak about a specific situation.

3. The Golden Rule can be applied by asking an important series of questions.
   a. Love of God and love of neighbor are what the Law and the Prophets point to, so we ask ourselves, "What would be for God's glory in this situation?"
   b. We place ourselves in somebody else's situations, and then ask ourselves, "How would I want them to love me and serve me for the glory of God?"
4. The Golden Rule is not a worldly principle.
   a. The Golden Rule takes into consideration the application of the wisdom of God's Word to every situation.
   b. It is not merely thinking about how we would like to be treated but how we would like to treat others the way Christ treated us for God's glory.
5. When we apply the Golden Rule, we are applying the wisdom of God.
   a. We then begin to live the way the Father would want us to live.
   b. We begin to follow the example of Christ, counting others as more important than ourselves, even being prepared to die for them.

STUDY QUESTIONS

1. All condemning judgments warrant the condemnation of the Father.
   a. True
   b. False

2. Judgments can be both judgments of condemnation and judgments of _____ .
   a. Wisdom
   b. Application
   c. Discernment
   d. Understanding

3. The Golden Rule and the _____ are the guidelines of wisdom when determining how to apply Scripture to specific situations.
   a. Proverbs
   b. Parables
   c. *Shema*
   d. Law

4. Exercising the wisdom of God is not possible in circumstances where Scripture does not explicitly speak.
   a. True
   b. False

5. Jesus uses the parable of the _____ to condemn the judgments of the Pharisees.
   a. Lost coin
   b. Lost sheep
   c. Prodigal son
   d. All of the above

6. The teaching of _____ on wisdom strongly parallels Jesus' teaching on wisdom in the Sermon on the Mount.
   a. Paul
   b. Peter
   c. James
   d. Jude

DISCUSSION QUESTIONS

1. How does knowledge of God as Father deliver us from condemning others?

2. As Christians we are frequently required to make judgments and decisions. In light of this, what did Jesus mean when He said, "Judge not" (Matt. 7:1)?

3. What important lesson does the Golden Rule teach us about applying Scripture?

4. How will practicing spiritual discernment help you in evangelism?

12

Ultimate Choices

INTRODUCTION

Jesus closes the Sermon on the Mount by revealing that He is the only way and our sure foundation. In this final lesson, Dr. Ferguson teaches us how judgment has eternal significance and is essential when determining which way to go, from whom to learn, and on what to build our lives.

LESSON OBJECTIVES

1. To arm believers with principles by which they can make ultimate choices
2. To provide tests that help identify false teachers
3. To point to Christ exclusively as our one and only foundation

SCRIPTURE READING

He drew me up from the pit of destruction, out of the miry bog, and set my feet upon a rock, making my steps secure.

—Psalm 40:2

LECTURE OUTLINE

A. Jesus moves from teaching about judgment as condemnation and discernment to teaching about ultimate choices.

1. The chapters of the Sermon on the Mount can be summed by the words *fulfillment*, *Father*, and *judgment*.
   a. The word *judgment* has shades of meaning.
   b. Jesus teaches us that we must avoid judgment as condemnation and practice judgment as discernment.
2. Judgment is necessary to navigate situations that the Bible doesn't directly speak about—the context of the Golden Rule.

      a. *Adiaphora* is a technical term for things that are indifferent, but the Christian is never indifferent about the choices that must be made.

      b. The Golden Rule is a principle that ultimately aims for God's glory and forces us to consider what is the best way to serve someone.

      c. This means that Christians do let people live in a way that leads to destruction.

B. Jesus uses the illustration of the narrow and the broad road to teach that there are only two ways to live.

   1. The two roads magnify the importance of judgment in the ultimate choices we make.

      a. As we stand in the crossroads of our lives, there is a narrow road and there is a broad road.

      b. There are plenty of people on the broad road and the narrow road looks hard, so we instinctively think the broad road is the right way.

      c. Our judgments are always being tested by the choices we make in life, but we must look and see where these two roads lead.

      d. Jesus emphasizes the destinations of these two roads as that which should inform our choices—destruction or life?

   2. In the Christian life, temptation seeks to deceive us.

      a. Temptation does not want us to focus on the long term or the destinations to which our choices will lead.

      b. Temptation wants us to focus on the short term and our relationships with others as opposed to our relationship with Christ.

      c. Considering where our choices ultimately lead is a principle that needs to inform our lives.

   3. The two roads illustrate the exclusivity of Christ.

      a. People who only think of Jesus as a great teacher have difficulty with this area of the Sermon on the Mount.

      b. Jesus is plainly teaching that there are only two ways to live—one to destruction, one to life—and this exclusivity offends them.

   4. The offense of the gospel is the exclusivity of the Lord Jesus Christ as the only Savior.

      a. The contemporary world is filled with the exclusive claims like those found in advertisements or news programs.

      b. No one would reject the one and only cure for a disease, and yet people often reject Christ based on His exclusivity.

   5. People who reject Christ are not able to see the depth of their sickness.

      a. In his *Cur Deus Homo* ("Why Did God Become Man?"), Anselm of Canterbury stresses the importance of understanding the full weight of sin as the starting point for recognizing our need for a remedy.

      b. As long as people think that they can somehow cure themselves, they will never see the beauty of Jesus Christ as the exclusive antidote.

c. God promises that He is able to save those who come to Him through Jesus Christ, no matter how spiritually sick, to the uttermost.

C. Jesus teaches us that judgment is required to determine which teachers and leaders we will follow.
1. Jesus underlines the necessity of judgment as discernment in determining which teachers we will follow.
   a. Jesus knows that false prophets do not announce themselves as such, so it is important to be able to identify a wolf in sheep's clothing.
   b. Charlatans can take advantage only of unsuspecting people.
2. Jesus gives us a test by which we can identify false teachers: "You will recognize them by their fruits" (Matt. 7:20).
   a. A teacher should remind us of Jesus in speech and character.
   b. Spiritual fruit, especially in the New Testament, is first and foremost likeness to Christ.
3. We also need to consider the fruit of those who are influenced by a teacher.
   a. People often develop the same personality traits as their teachers.
   b. The fruit of a ministry should free people to live to the glory of God.
   c. The gospel will always produce the fruit of the Spirit (Gal. 5:22–23).
4. "Not everyone who says to me, 'Lord, Lord,' will enter the kingdom" (Matt. 7:21) is another test by which we can discern false teachers.
   a. Jesus is teaching us to distinguish between mere impressionability and the grace that draws us to Jesus Christ.
   b. It is possible for a person to preach eloquently and yet not be a true believer.
5. The gifts we possess are meant to direct others to Christ and not ourselves.
   a. When a person draws attention to his gifts, he is speaking gracelessly and not gracefully.
   b. Christ sent out the seventy-two, and Judas returned among them rejoicing, "Lord, even the demons are subject to us in your name" (Luke 10:17).
   c. Jesus may have had Judas in mind when He replied, "Rejoice that your names are written in heaven" (Luke 10:20).
   d. Judas could not even rejoice that something beautiful was done for Jesus when He was anointed with perfume at Bethany.
   e. False teachers draw people's eyes away from Jesus Christ to their own gifts and ministry.

D. Jesus teaches us that we need to make judgments about the foundation on which we will build our lives.
1. We must decide which way we will go, what teachers we will learn from, and what the true foundation of our lives is.
   a. Christ illustrates this final decision by comparing two men—one who built his house on a rock and another who built his house on sand.

2. It is utter foolishness to build on anything but Jesus Christ.
    a. Understanding this is wisdom that a child can possess but that can be utterly lacking in a mature adult.
    b. We cannot build our lives on something based on convenience.
    c. It is only those who build their lives on Jesus Christ who will stand in the final judgment.
3. When Jesus finished preaching, the crowd was astonished with the authority with which He preached.
    a. This sets up the rest of the gospel of Matthew with the question of how people will respond to Him.
    b. It is one thing to be impressed with His authority, another to grasp the significance of what He is saying, and even another to bow to Him as Lord and Savior.
    c. The Sermon on the Mount ends where the Christian life begins: Are you building on the sand, or are you building on Christ the Rock?

STUDY QUESTIONS

1. The final chapter of the Sermon on the Mount can be summarized by the word

    _____ .
    a. Transformation
    b. Fulfillment
    c. Judgment
    d. Father

2. *Adiaphora* is a term that describes the way Christians think of the areas that the Bible doesn't specifically address.
    a. True
    b. False

3. The offense of the gospel in our own time is the _____ of the Lord and Savior Jesus Christ.
    a. Power
    b. Wisdom
    c. Inclusivity
    d. Exclusivity

4. False teachers are hard to identify because they do not resemble the Lord Jesus Christ.
    a. True
    b. False

5. Understanding our sin is a foundational starting place according to _____ *Cur Deus Homo*.
   a. Boso's
   b. Calvin's
   c. Anselm's
   d. Luther's

6. It is only after years of Christian growth that one can recognize that Jesus Christ is the Rock on which we are to build our lives.
   a. True
   b. False

DISCUSSION QUESTIONS

1. What is the most important consideration in the face of temptation?

2. Why is it important to understand the weight of our sin?

3. How has Jesus taught us to identify false teachers? What qualities did Judas share with false teachers?

4. Why do you think the exclusive claims of Christ are often received with offense?

Answer Key for Study Questions

Lesson 1	**Lesson 5**	**Lesson 9**
1. C	1. B	1. A
2. B	2. A	2. D
3. B	3. B	3. C
4. B	4. B	4. A
5. B	5. D	5. D
6. D	6. D	6. D

Lesson 2	**Lesson 6**	**Lesson 10**
1. C	1. B	1. D
2. B	2. D	2. B
3. B	3. D	3. D
4. C	4. C	4. C
5. D	5. B	5. D
6. C	6. D	6. B

Lesson 3	**Lesson 7**	**Lesson 11**
1. B	1. B	1. A
2. A	2. D	2. C
3. B	3. C	3. C
4. B	4. D	4. B
5. D	5. A	5. D
6. A	6. D	6. C

Lesson 4	**Lesson 8**	**Lesson 12**
1. D	1. D	1. C
2. D	2. B	2. B
3. A	3. C	3. D
4. C	4. C	4. B
5. B	5. B	5. C
6. B	6. D	6. B